# A is for Astronaut

## *Blasting Through the Alphabet*

Written by Astronaut Clayton Anderson and Illustrated by Scott Brundage

With the formation of the National Aeronautics and Space Administration (NASA) in 1958, the seven men designated as the Mercury astronauts would be the first Americans ever selected to venture into the unknown of outer space. Described by NASA simply as Group 1, they were also known as the Mercury 7 or the Original 7.

These military fighter-pilots-turned-astronauts (M. Scott Carpenter, Gordon Cooper Jr., John H. Glenn Jr., Gus Grissom, Wally M. Schirra Jr., Deke Slayton, and Alan B. Shepard) became instant American heroes.

Since that first group of astronauts, approximately 350 astronaut candidates, making up 22 different groups, have been selected to be United States astronauts. All astronaut groups are given nicknames, like Penguins, 8-Balls, Turtles, and Bugs!

A a

A is for Astronaut,
the bravest of souls.
They fly into space
and assume many roles.
They pilot, they spacewalk,
and they even cut hair.
But seeing Earth from our orbit—
that will cause them to stare!

B is for Blastoff, a powerful thing!
When those engines are fired, it'll make your ears ring.
There is smoke—and vibration—as we launch into space.
And we do it with flair, with excitement and grace!

The launch of the space shuttle was an amazing sight to see. The shuttle, powered by two solid rocket motors and three space shuttle main engines, generated nearly 7 million pounds of thrust at liftoff!

The shuttle "stack" (the shuttle, its boosters, and orange fuel tank) traveled at more than 120 miles an hour by the time it cleared the launch pad. The blastoff is simply a well-controlled explosion.

Just six minutes after liftoff, the shuttle is moving so fast that everything on board will weigh nearly three times more than it did on Earth. Then, 2.5 minutes later, when the main engines cut off, everything will be floating. Welcome to outer space! Please enjoy the view!

Bb

The Capsule's important, and it starts with a C.
It's a tiny compartment, much too crowded for me.
Our heroes will live there, through all of their flight.
They'll eat, sleep, and work in a space that's quite tight!

# Cc

Early space capsules were very small and compact. The Mercury program capsule could carry a single astronaut, and Alan Shepard was the first American to launch into space. Later, Project Gemini's capsule took two astronauts. For the Apollo moon missions, the capsule was large enough for three space fliers, and the space shuttles could carry a crew of seven.

Today NASA hopes to send humans back to the moon and then on to Mars. To do that, they are building a huge rocket called the Space Launch System (SLS) and a space capsule called the Orion Multi-Purpose Crew Vehicle. Orion, shaped like a big gumdrop, is designed to carry a crew of two to six astronauts to space.

Every time we send satellites, probes, or humans into space, we are trying to learn. Valuable information is gathered and later reviewed by talented scientists and engineers. This data helps us gain new understanding, leading to updated concepts and better equipment, expanding our knowledge of the universe.

Spaceships gather enormous amounts of data using their computers. From things like vehicle speeds and temperatures to heart rates of astronauts and pictures of Earth, every single piece of information is reviewed and studied.

Many useful products have resulted from information gathered by our space program. For example, our smartphones are possible because of satellites and updated computer technology. Portable tools powered by rechargeable batteries were "born" during the Apollo program when astronauts used similar tools to collect moon rocks. Invisible braces used to straighten teeth, sunglasses, Super Soaker squirt guns, and foam gliders are just a few examples of things that came from our study of space.

Dd

For engineers and scientists, knowledge is key.
And D stands for Data, information we need.
Be it numbers or symbols, we must send it to Earth,
for it's there that trained people will determine its worth.

The Milky Way galaxy is the home of our solar system and possibly many others. Named because it looks like a milky-white band stretching far across the night sky, it is home to billions and billions of stars.

The Milky Way is shaped like a big spiral disk and is rotating ever so slowly within our universe (imagine a spinning pinwheel). It is also moving slowly away from the center of the universe, much like the ripples in a pond when a stone is tossed into the water.

The Milky Way contains over one hundred billion other planets, some of which may be very similar to our Earth. We call them "exoplanets," and maybe one day we'll find one just like ours!

# Gg

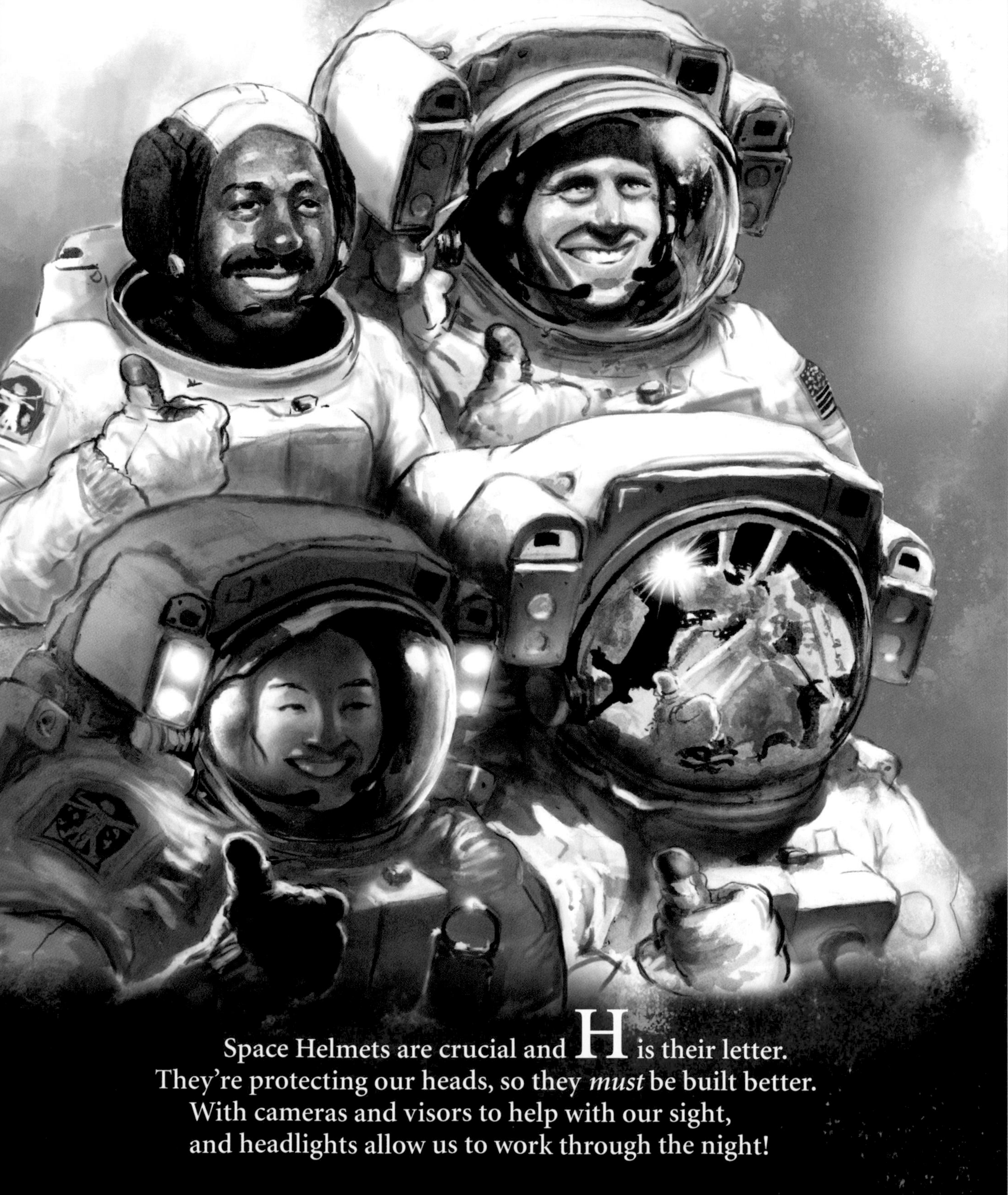

Space Helmets are crucial and **H** is their letter.
They're protecting our heads, so they *must* be built better.
With cameras and visors to help with our sight,
and headlights allow us to work through the night!

The helmet is a key part of any space suit, and it must form a tight seal with the upper part of the suit.

To help astronauts communicate with everyone, they wear a special cap inside the helmet. The cap has microphones and speakers. It also helps to protect the top of the astronaut's head. The helmet has a clear visor through which astronauts can see while they are working and moving about in the vacuum of outer space.

If work is being done in the dark (when the sun is blocked by the Earth), the helmet has special lights that let the astronauts see. When the sun comes back out, we pull down our sunshield, which acts like a big pair of sunglasses and makes the front of the helmet look bright gold. TV cameras let folks on the ground see what we see while we work!

Hh

When we zoom 'round the Earth, there's an angle we need.
It's very important, not related to speed.
Called Inclination, it starts with an I,
and it dictates over which part of Earth we will fly!

# Ii

A spacecraft can fly around the Earth horizontally (like on a tabletop), vertically (up and down like a carnival's Ferris wheel), or something in between. Whatever the angle is, NASA engineers call that the mission's orbital inclination.

If we were to fly horizontally around the Earth, we would essentially be following the equator, and our inclination angle would be zero degrees. If we chose to do a polar orbit that allowed us to fly over the north and south poles, that inclination would be 90 degrees.

For the space station, we choose something in between to allow many different countries to launch their spaceships and reach the station. That inclination is about 52 degrees. If you look at a globe and find 52 degrees above the equator and 52 degrees below the equator, we know that the space station will fly over all parts of the Earth between those lines. Check it out!

When astronauts perform space walks they may have to remove old, excess, or broken equipment. Depending on size, they may bring the material back inside the space station for storage or they may return it to Earth for repair. But sometimes we "take out the trash," or throw the items out into space, allowing Earth's gravity to pull them toward the ground. This is called a jettison. The object will burn up from friction with the Earth's atmospheric layers as gravity pulls it to the planet's surface.

Jettisons are carefully planned. The direction the objects are thrown and how hard we throw them are very important. In space, things don't travel in a perfectly straight line; they move in circles or orbits, like long arcs or curves. Since we don't want large objects to make it all the way to the ground—they might injure someone—it's important we throw them so they will burn up. We also don't want to throw them in a direction that might lead them to collide with other objects, like our spaceship!

To Jettison means we throw something away,
like broken equipment
or an old solar array.
Its letter is J, and it's like tossing out trash,
which will hit the Earth's atmosphere and burn up in a flash!

The 35th president,
his last name started with **K**.
John F. Kennedy was a man
who had so much to say.
He challenged our nation
to do things that were hard,
saying, "We choose to go to the moon,"
where our astronauts starred.

United States President John F. Kennedy was key in the development of our nation's space program. He challenged America to put a man on the moon and return him safely to Earth within the next ten years. With such a short time to accomplish his challenge, thousands of Americans worked very hard to turn his dream into reality.

On July 20, 1969, humans landed on the moon's surface; the very next day, astronaut Neil Armstrong became the first person to step down onto another world. His footprint is still there!

In honor of President Kennedy and his brilliant vision, the Florida base we use for launching our many rockets, astronauts, and spacecraft is called the Kennedy Space Center (KSC). The center also serves as a wildlife sanctuary and is home to thousands of animals, including birds, alligators, and snakes.

After any space mission, we return to the Earth.
We plan it in detail for all that it's worth.
A safe Landing is needed, and it starts with an **L**.
When we're back here on Earth, oh, what stories we'll tell!

Spacecraft landings happen in many different ways. For example, the space shuttles landed like an airplane, gliding to the runway before touching down gently. Once at a full stop, the crew exited the shuttle to the runway, where a special bus waited to carry them to their families.

When NASA uses space capsules, they parachute softly to Earth and land near a preplanned spot in either the Atlantic or the Pacific Ocean. There they will be met by a United States Navy ship, a helicopter to retrieve the capsule, and scuba divers to retrieve the astronauts.

Russian space capsules also use parachutes, but they usually land in a big flat field of grass. Future capsule landings may bring astronauts right back to where they launched from!

L l

M Rocks flying through space leaving bright yellow trails
need an M 'cause they're Meteors with very long tails.
When they get close to our planet, with atmosphere near,
they will burn up quite quickly and —poof— disappear.

# M m

Meteoroids and asteroids are solid objects—think: rocks—moving through space. Asteroids can be very large, but meteoroids are usually much smaller and may be as tiny as a speck of dust. Nearly all meteoroids come from chunks of rock that break off from asteroids or comets located in the asteroid belt that stretches between the planets of Mars and Jupiter. When a meteoroid enters the Earth's atmosphere, the intense friction between the atmospheric layers and the rock creates incredible amounts of heat, and the meteoroid begins to burn and glow. It is now called a meteor—or shooting star. If a small part of one of these meteors survives through the fiery entry of Earth's atmosphere, it is then called a meteorite.

Scientists on Earth become extremely excited when they are able to recover meteorites on the Earth's surface. In fact, many scientists journey to Antarctica in search of these informative pieces of rock. We can learn much about the beginning of our solar system—and even our universe—by studying the composition of these tiny stones.

NASA was formed in 1958 by then-president Dwight D. Eisenhower. Its goal is to better understand our planet and solar system, as well as to learn more about the origin of our universe. Most people know that NASA sends astronauts into space, but developing robotic space probes, launching research satellites, and studying aerodynamics are also important efforts performed by NASA. Today, NASA is headquartered in our nation's capital, Washington, DC.

NASA represents the best of both human and robotic space programs, as well as providing key contributions in aviation. From communication satellites orbiting high above our planet to airport runways around the world, NASA continues to influence the design and development of technologies that make air and space travel safer, more efficient, and more affordable. It won't be long until you will be able to purchase a ticket for your own personal journey into space!

# Nn

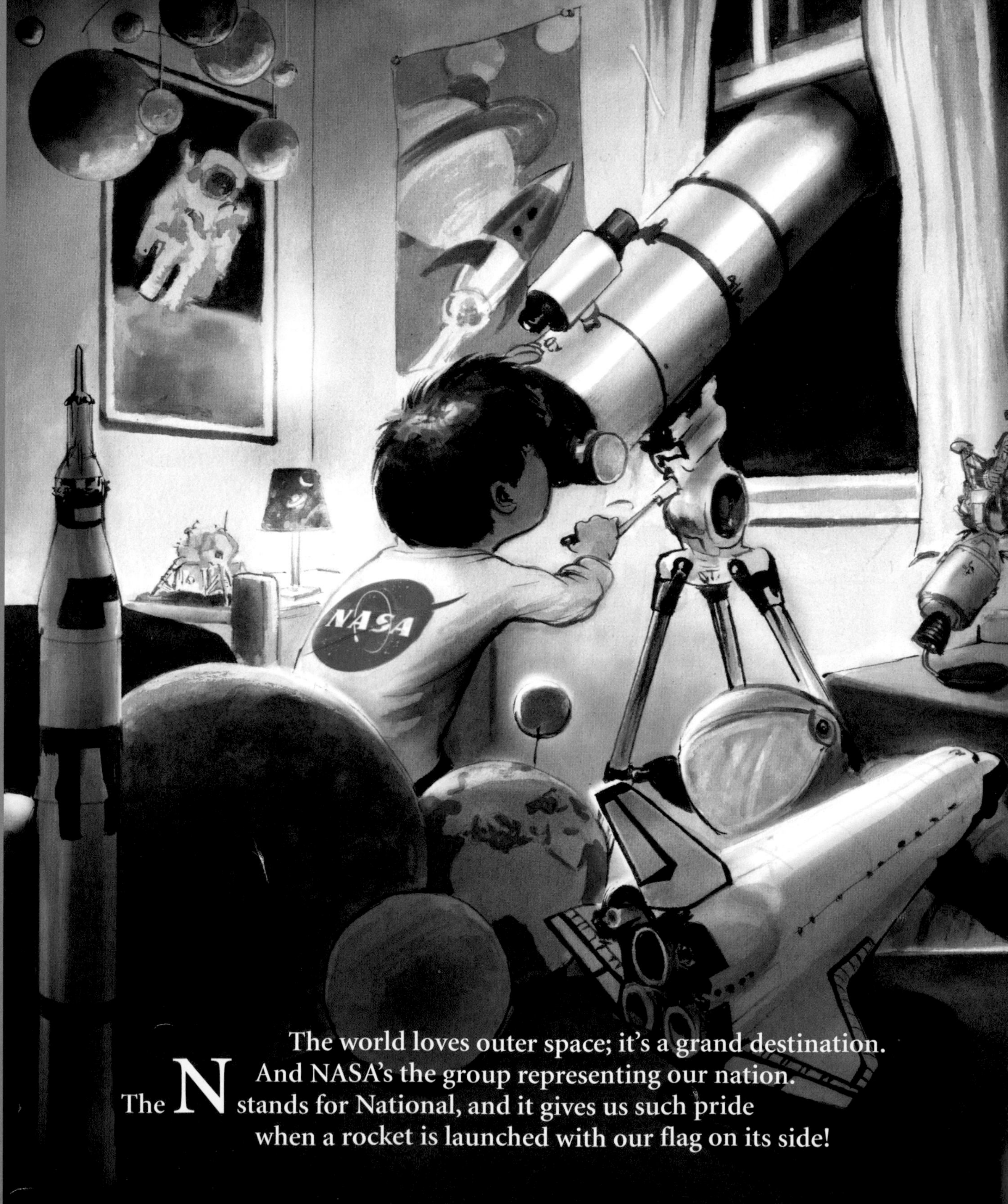


The world loves outer space; it's a grand destination.
And NASA's the group representing our nation.
The N stands for National, and it gives us such pride
when a rocket is launched with our flag on its side!

Q is for Quasar, an incredible star.
Quasars appear faint and red,
as their distance is far.
They send X-rays and light
to all corners of space,
but their pull is so strong,
not much light will escape.

# Qq

Quasars are bright masses of energy and light that are constantly sending out radio, X-ray, and light waves. The name *quasar* is short for "quasi-stellar radio source" or "quasi-stellar object."

Quasars are extremely distant objects in our universe. They are so far away from our Milky Way galaxy we can barely see them, even with special telescopes. While they are one of the brightest objects in our universe, they appear as faint red stars to us here on Earth.

A quasar is thought to be an incredibly large object—also known as a black hole—surrounded by a flat, Frisbee-like cloud of gas. This gas cloud spins rapidly around the quasar and gradually gets sucked into the black hole by its super-strong gravity. It's possible that stars, and even small galaxies, get sucked in too. When that happens, everything crashes together, and a gigantic explosion shoots out energy and light, called a flare. When scientists are able to see these quasars, the light has traveled so far for so long that we are actually looking back in time. Whoa!

# Rr

**R** is for Rendezvous,
meaning in space we will meet.
To bring two ships together
can be quite the feat.
Using thrust from our engines,
smart computers, and plans,
if we do it correctly, crews can finally shake hands!

NASA engineers invented and perfected the concept of space rendezvous in the 1960s. The word comes from the French language and means "to meet at a certain time and place." This "meeting" gets a tad bit more complicated when it's scheduled to happen in outer space.

Consider the much-simplified example of a football game where the coach has called for a pass play. In order for the pass play to be successful, the quarterback must throw the football (spaceship one) to the pass receiver (spaceship two) who will catch the ball. The quarterback throws the ball to where the receiver is going to be—not where he is at the instant he makes the throw. When the ball finally arrives and the receiver makes the catch, the play is a success! This is similar to the way spaceships will dock, or meet, in space.

Working outside in space is sure to impress.
We call it a Space Walk, and its letter is S.
Floating weightless, with tools and a bulky white suit,
we can fix and install things—it's really a hoot!

Astronauts perform space walks for many reasons. They can install new equipment or fix things that are broken. An American space walk usually lasts about 6.5 hours, and the astronauts work in pairs to help keep each other safe. Big jobs need them to work together as a two-person team, but sometimes they do smaller jobs individually, always talking to one another to maintain awareness and check in.

When going into and working in space, different suits are used for different tasks. The suit worn during launch and landing is called the ACES (Advanced Crew Escape Space Suit System) suit and is bright orange in color. It protects astronauts in the event of an emergency situation.

For space walks, the suit is quite different. Much heavier and colored bright white, it becomes your own personal spaceship and tool storage device while you work in the vacuum of space.

Ss

To reach space destinations, one thing is a must.
It frees us from gravity,
and we call it Thrust.
Starting with T,
it's the force we will need
as a fiery rocket gives our ship plenty of speed.

# Tt

It takes a lot of energy to put an object into space. That's because the Earth has gravity, which pulls everything down to the ground, including our very heavy rocket and spaceship. When we launch, we use rocket fuels like hydrogen and oxygen to create a big, controlled explosion. The power created by this explosion as it fires out from an engine nozzle is our thrust, the force that pushes us up into space.

In order to get into an orbit circling the Earth, we have to reach a very high speed. Called orbital velocity, the speed of something flying in space is about 17,500 miles per hour. If we don't fly that fast, we will eventually fall back to Earth.

So the explosion we use to generate the needed thrust has to be big enough to "lift" our heavy rocket up into the sky and propel our spaceship to reach that enormous speed. It really is rocket science!

**U** is for Universe, the place we explore.
Using spaceships and rockets, we are searching for more.
New planets, new worlds, maybe beings like us;
if we are to find them, then continue we must!

Since humans have been on Earth, we have been exploring. From the Vikings to historical explorers like Christopher Columbus, Ferdinand Magellan, and Vasco da Gama, all risked their lives exploring our Earth. As they ventured away from their safe, secure homes they longed to find new worlds and adventures. In America, colonial settlers moved west in search of better lives, exploring the vast territory that would one day become the United States.

Today, we explore in new ways. We now explore up and out—into our universe. We sail not across water, but through a dangerous, endless vacuum of space. By sending astronauts and data-gathering probes away from our planet, we make wonderful discoveries and develop new ideas and technology. From information on our climate to useful devices like power tools, smartphones, and health equipment, this exploration continues to improve life on Earth.

Uu

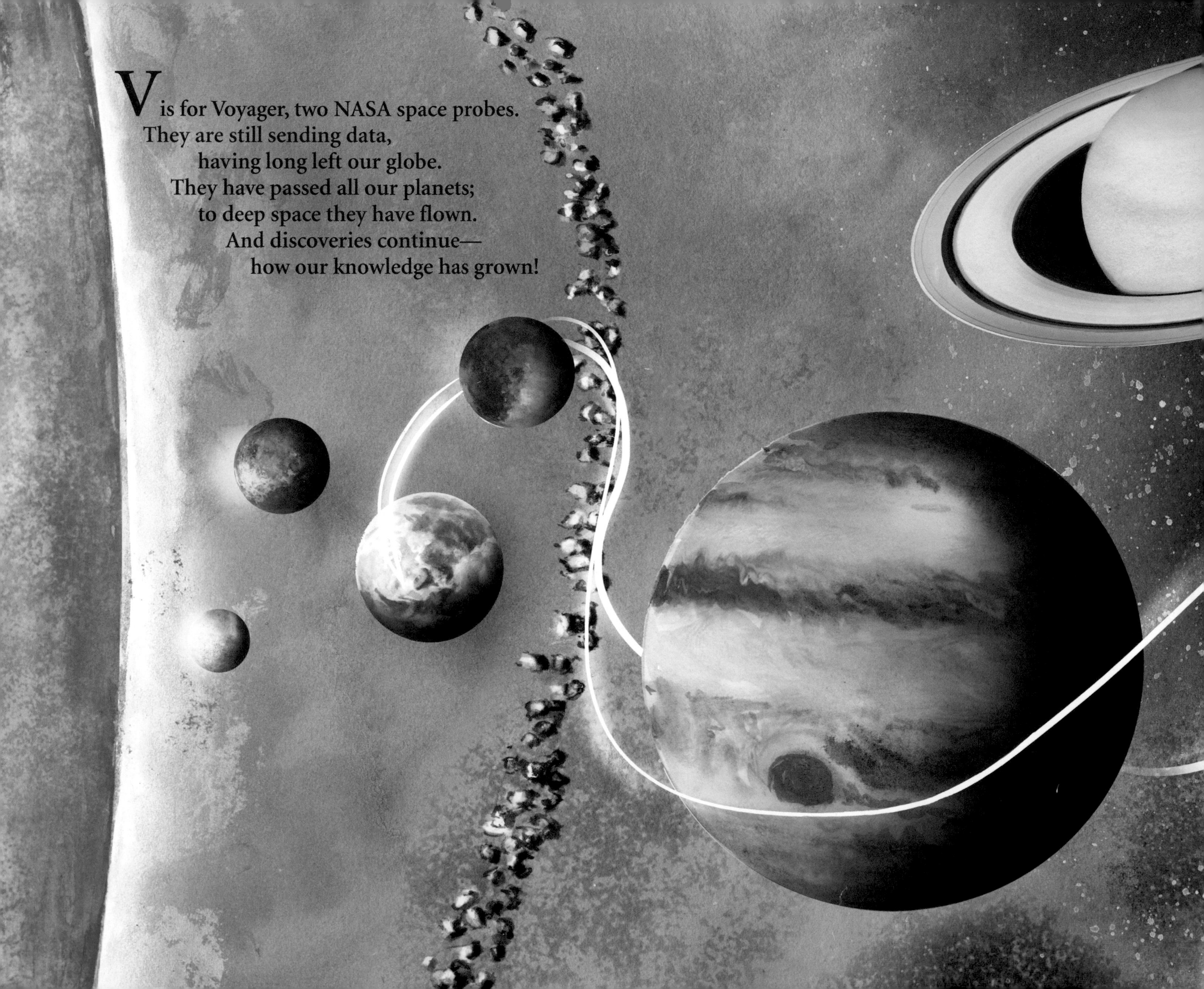

V is for Voyager, two NASA space probes.
They are still sending data,
having long left our globe.
They have passed all our planets;
to deep space they have flown.
And discoveries continue—
how our knowledge has grown!

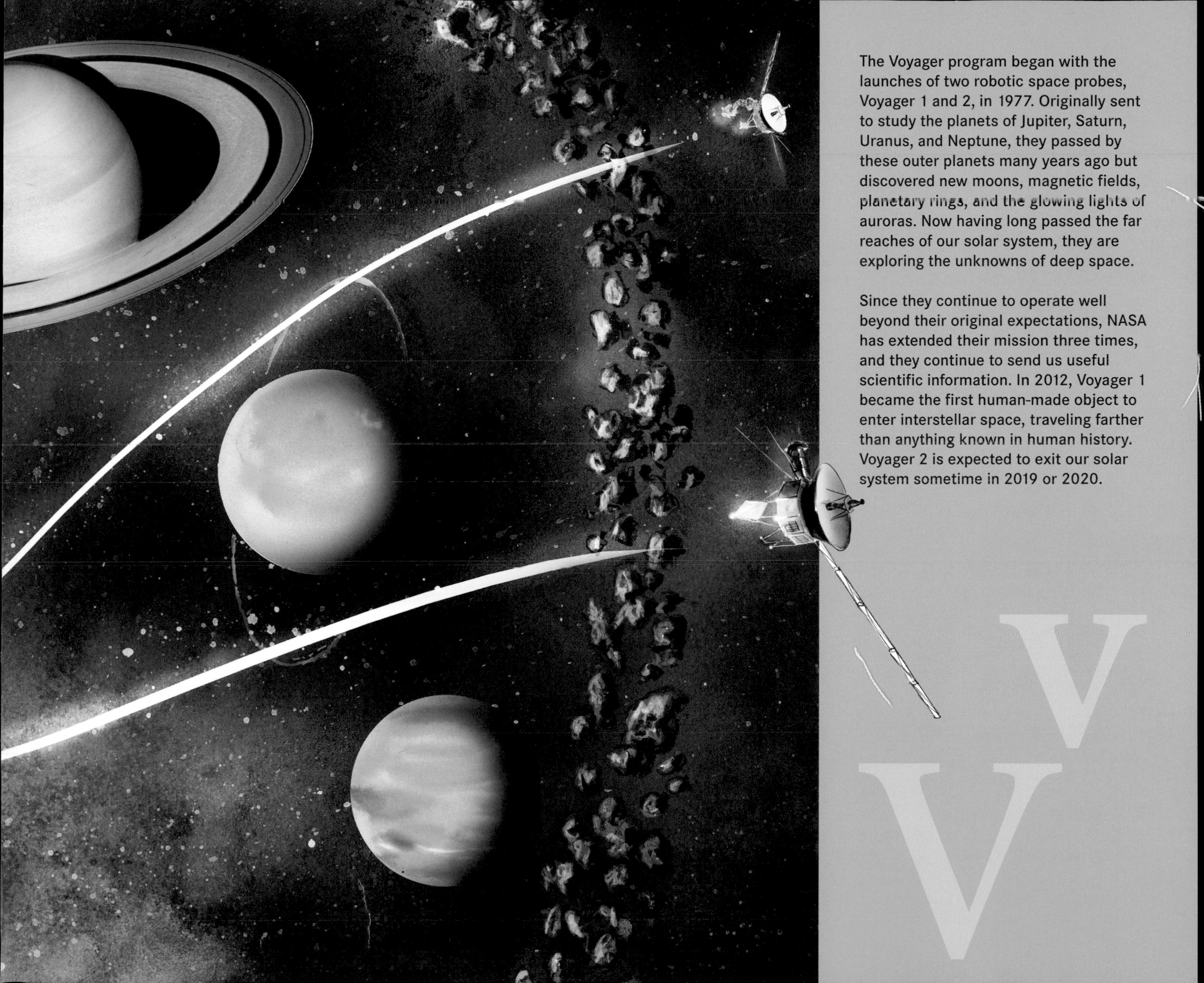

The Voyager program began with the launches of two robotic space probes, Voyager 1 and 2, in 1977. Originally sent to study the planets of Jupiter, Saturn, Uranus, and Neptune, they passed by these outer planets many years ago but discovered new moons, magnetic fields, planetary rings, and the glowing lights of auroras. Now having long passed the far reaches of our solar system, they are exploring the unknowns of deep space.

Since they continue to operate well beyond their original expectations, NASA has extended their mission three times, and they continue to send us useful scientific information. In 2012, Voyager 1 became the first human-made object to enter interstellar space, traveling farther than anything known in human history. Voyager 2 is expected to exit our solar system sometime in 2019 or 2020.

V v

As we climb high into space,
Wind is always a force.
Beginning with W, it may blow us off course.
The rocket's computers will just move us a bit,
so our target is always
the place we will hit.

For every launch, technical experts must take a hard look at the weather. These experts analyze winds and forecasts, looking for issues that could impact a successful launch. Not only do they check the launch site for the conditions before and during the launch, they must sometimes check additional sites and later times. This was very important when the space shuttle was flying, because emergency landing sites might have been needed. The shuttle would not launch if the weather at one of its emergency sites was expected to be bad at the time they might need to land there. Launch would be delayed until conditions improved.

Understanding the effects that wind might have on a launch is perhaps the greatest concern for success. As a rocket launches and moves higher into the atmosphere, winds can change dramatically in both force (how hard they are blowing) and direction (which way they are blowing). The rocket must be able to deal with these changes to stay on its flight path. Today, advanced computers are able to measure the winds and adjust the vehicle's flight direction and speed as it heads for its orbital target.

Ww

X-rays are invisible;
we can't see them on Earth.
Their letter is X and they have serious worth.
Harnessed correctly, they let doctors see
deep inside our bodies where problems may be.

Cosmic X-rays are a powerful form of light energy that cannot be seen with our eyes. They were first discovered shooting from our sun in the 1940s, and scientists and astronomers later found that X-rays also come from deep space. Since X-rays are absorbed by our atmosphere, the science called X-ray astronomy must be performed in space, using equipment like balloons, rockets, and space satellites taken to high altitudes.

The study of cosmic X-rays is important to understanding the formation of our universe. By looking at the sky with instruments detecting X-rays, scientists may find answers as to how the universe began, how it is changing, and perhaps what it will be like in the future.

Space station astronauts have a system to tell them when things may be going wrong. It's called Caution and Warning. Alarms can be red or yellow, and the crew will hear a different sound for each so they can tell them apart. Red alarms are called emergencies and include fires, dangerous spills, or a leak of air or oxygen. Yellow alarms are called cautions, and they cover everything else. Cautions are not considered as serious as emergencies.

The flight controllers on the Mission Control Center team are able to look at each alarm and help the crew respond as needed. For yellow cautions, the team on the ground often handles everything. The crew may not even know that an alarm occurred! But if an emergency sounds, it's all hands on deck, and everyone works hard to make sure the crew and the spacecraft are safe.

Yy

In spaceships, the color Yellow, with a Y, is well-known.
It means there's a caution with an alarm and a tone.
But the crew won't be upset, nor scared nor afraid;
it's not usually a crisis, and the ground will give aid.

# Z

While living on the space station, astronauts follow the same time zone as London, England. This time reference is known around the world as Zulu Time or Greenwich Mean Time (GMT). Since the exploration of space is now done by countries around the world, we need a common time that everyone can use. GMT represents a kind of "in the middle" point for all the countries involved with the space station program (Europe, Japan, USA, Russia, and Canada).

Astronauts usually wake up at about 0600 in the morning, and go to bed at about 1030 at night. Their workday is roughly 6.5 hours long and they're required to do 2.5 hours of exercise. The remaining hours of the day are spent eating, cleaning up, or working at their laptop computers. Most astronauts don't go to sleep at 1030 though—they stay up late watching TV and movies, gazing out the windows at Earth, or sending email!

Z is for Zulu, which represents time.
It's our reference to England, when London's clocks chime.
As we fly 'round the Earth, folks must know our day's plan,
so we all set our watches to match that time span.

*To Susan, the center of my universe.*
*For my children, Cole and Sutton, their children . . . and their children's children . . .*
*And to Marcia Jussel, and those with vision.*
*— Clayton*

*To my dad, who gave me the confidence to shoot for stars.*
*— Scott*



Sleeping Bear Press™

2395 South Huron Parkway, Suite 200
Ann Arbor, MI 48104
www.sleepingbearpress.com

Printed and bound in the United States.

Library of Congress Cataloging-in-Publication Data

Names: Anderson, Clayton C., 1959- author. | Brundage, Scott, illustrator.
Title: A is for astronaut : blasting through the alphabet / written by Clayton Anderson ; illustrated by Scott Brundage.
Description: Ann Arbor, MI : Sleeping Bear Press, [2018] | Audience: Age 5-10.
Identifiers: LCCN 2017029870 | ISBN 9781585363964
Subjects: LCSH: Outer space--Exploration--Juvenile literature. | English language--Alphabet--Juvenile literature.
Classification: LCC TL793 .A51485 2018 | DDC 629.45--dc23
LC record available at https://lccn.loc.gov/2017029870
9 8 7 6 5 4 3